Lynda Field is a trained counsellor and psychotherapist who specializes in personal and group development. The author of the bestselling *60 Ways to Feel Amazing*, *Creating Self-Esteem* and *The Self-Esteem Workbook*, she lives in Essex, England.

by the same author

60 Ways to
HEAL YOUR LIFE

LYNDA FIELD

E L E M E N T

Shaftesbury, Dorset • Boston, Massachusetts
Melbourne, Victoria

DEDICATED TO MY WONDERFUL MOTHER, BARBARA GORONWY

© Element Books Limited 1999
Text © Lynda Field 1999

First published in the UK in 1999 by
Element Books Limited, Shaftesbury, Dorset SP7 8BP

Published in the USA in 1999 by
Element Books, Inc.
160 North Washington Street, Boston, MA 02114

Published in Australia in 1999 by
Element Books and distributed
by Penguin Australia Limited
487 Maroondah Highway, Ringwood, Victoria 3134

Illustrations by Alison Campbell
Cover design by Mark Slader
Design by Roger Lightfoot
Typeset by Bournemouth Colour Press, Parkstone, Poole
Printed and bound in Great Britain by Biddles Ltd, Guildford &
King's Lynn

British Library Cataloguing in Publication
data available

Library of Congress Cataloging in Publication
data available

ISBN 1–86204–308–6

Contents

Introduction

Life is a precious gift, miraculous and amazing, but we are not always able to appreciate this miracle fully. When we face obstacles and difficulties our lives can become such a struggle that we lose touch with the amazingness of it all.

When things are getting you down and everything feels like hard work you need to bring back the wonder into your life; to fill yourself with inspiration and hope; to re-energize yourself and to strengthen your self-belief so that you can find creative solutions to your problems and regain control of your life.

This book is full of ways to bring back the magic into your life. Choose the ones that most attract you and give them a try. All the techniques are simple and practical and tried and tested many times.

Always remember that you are a special and amazing person with unique talents and strengths. Use the techniques in this book to help you to heal your life and feel as amazing as you truly are.

Lynda Field

Lynda Field

Nurture yourself for a day

1 Nurture Yourself for a Day

What does it mean to nurture yourself?
Do you nurture yourself?
How do you treat yourself?

Think of the way you would treat a small helpless child. If
this child was hungry, you would feed him; if he was
crying, you would comfort him; if he made a mistake, you
would forgive him; if he fell over, you would pick him up
and help him back to his feet. You would encourage this
child in every way you knew. When he falls over, you don't
yell at him. If he drops a toy, you don't criticize him. He is
free to make mistakes because this is how he learns. You
know that this child will develop through love and support;
he will not develop and learn if he is abused. Of course you
treat him well, he is only a child and deserves your
supportive love and care.

Answer the following questions.

- Do you treat yourself in this caring way?
- Do you love and encourage yourself?
- Do you help yourself up when you fall and comfort
  yourself when you are sad?
- Do you forgive yourself when you make a mistake?

We find it so difficult to treat ourselves in this loving and
nurturing way. Decide to nuture yourself for a day and see
how it goes. Say the following affirmation to yourself
throughout the day.

AFFIRMATION: *I deserve love and care.*

Try to make sure that every thought or action of the day is one that supports and encourages you. Remember how you would treat that small child – well, treat yourself in exactly the same way. Nuture yourself for a day and the habit may grow.

Create peace of mind

2 Create Peace of Mind

Being at peace does not mean losing touch with reality and escaping into a dream world, it means exactly the opposite. As soon as our mind stops whirling we are able to tap into a great source of energy. When our minds are at peace we feel harmonious and balanced, we are able to communicate well and make effective decisions, we feel relaxed and in control and life is a joy. Try the following two exercises to help you to create peace of mind.

EXERCISE 1 – MEMORIZE PEACEFULNESS

The next time you see a beautiful peaceful scene, close your eyes and commit the view to memory. This is much easier than it sounds, it just takes a bit of practice. Draw on this memory when you need to bring some peace into your life. Make a collection of peaceful scenes and memories and replay them whenever you feel the need. When we tap into visions of peace and harmony we re-experience the positive feelings. Let the pictures cross your mind, they are like a healing balm.

EXERCISE 2 – ACT INSTEAD OF REACTING

Peace comes when we take assertive charge of our lives instead of behaving like a passive victim. When a problem comes along, don't waste your energy worrying and getting upset and *re-acting*. Stop and face the problem and decide the best way to tackle it and then *act*. When we are dealing courageously with our lives we gain self-respect and peace of mind.

Try this two-fold approach. The visualization will work at the spiritual level and the assertive technique works at the behavioural level. Peace of mind allows us to realize our full creative and amazing potential. Realize your own potential.

Be an encourager

3   Be an Encourager

Who do you know who could do with some encouragement right now? Maybe it's you. One of the surest ways to give yourself hope is to inspire someone else. People have good intentions, they want to communicate and they want to be creative. These qualities may not always be obvious but be assured that they are always there (however deeply buried). So how can you be an encourager? Think of someone who encouraged you. What did they say? What did they do? The following exercise might help you with some ideas.

EXERCISE

1 Think of someone who encouraged and helped you to do your best. Write their name.

. . . .

2 How did they inspire you? What did they do to help you to succeed?

. . . .

3 How can you use these strategies to encourage someone else?

. . . .

Look around you and find someone who needs some inspiration. Encourage them to do what they can, rather than think about what they can't do. When you start to encourage another person something incredible happens – you feel encouraged yourself.

Bring your skeletons out of the closet

4 Bring Your Skeletons Out of the Closet

'Oh no,' I hear you say, 'I couldn't possibly tell of some of the things that I have done.' You know, one of the most important things that happens to people who come on my workshops is that they realize that we all have what we consider to be shameful secrets. You are not alone, everyone has thought and done things that they wished they hadn't, we all make mistakes. But if you have hidden these things away you are also carrying a burden of guilt and shame as well as fear (that they will be revealed). Open the closet. I'm not suggesting that you reveal all on national TV or even that you tell anyone. Just take a look at these things on your own, and as you look at them they will lose their mystery and power.

Yes, I did this, I've paid my price in guilt and now I can let go of it. And yes, I said that and it had a terrible effect. Maybe I could apologize to that person or just let it go, I have punished myself enough.

EXERCISE – BRINGING YOUR SKELETONS OUT OF THE CLOSET

If your closet is full of rattling, secret skeletons, then you are using up a lot of energy in just trying to keep that closet door shut (what if they should all come bursting out?). Take the following steps.

- Invite them out for an airing.
- Survey each one coolly.
- Remedy anything that you can.
- Let them rattle off in peace.

Your energy will increase and you will feel amazing.

Stop comparison shopping

5 Stop Comparison Shopping

Just watch those TV adverts! If only we use 'so and so' product we too will look as elegant/be as confident/sound as intelligent/be as thin/look as young/be as fit as … whom?

When we are feeling low we often compare ourselves unfavourably with others. We go 'comparison shopping' where we 'buy into' the concept of a comparative scale of self-worth:

> *I'm not as beautiful as …………… but I'm more beautiful than ……………*
> *I'm not clever enough/good enough to do that.*

Do you ever compare yourself with others? How do we know if we are clever/worthy/confident/beautiful/ happy/doing well/doing badly … etc?

No one else can be inside you. No one else can experience your self-satisfaction (or lack of it). Only you know what it feels like to be you. Stop comparison shopping, it will never do you any good because it will always keep you feeling negative and low in self-esteem. Every time you compare youself with someone else become aware of what you are doing and stop it! Say instead:

> *I am good enough.*

You are a special and unique person and you are irreplaceable. Remember to make positive affirmations about yourself and your life will become a positive experience.

Give your back a rest

6   Give Your Back a Rest

So many people suffer with backache. Poor posture, too much sitting and too little exercise can aggravate the problem. If you measure yourself when you get up and then measure at the end of your busy day you will have shrunk by as much as an inch. Gravity puts pressure on the discs between your vertebrate, muscles become shorter and joints become jammed together. No wonder we feel de-energized! Try to find a few minutes each day to allow your spine to lengthen, to loosen up your back muscles and recharge your batteries.

EXERCISE

1 Lie down on your back, upper arms resting on the floor and hands resting on your abdomen.

2 Support your head with a small cushion so that your head is in line with the rest of your body.

3 Pull up your legs, knees pointing to the ceiling. Keep your knees apart (about shoulder width) and your feet flat on the floor. Feel how this brings your lower back closer to the floor.

Rest like this for just a few minutes every day and feel the difference in your energy levels.

Go boldly

7 Go Boldly

What is worrying you? What are you afraid of? What is standing in your way? Our biggest fear is of fear itself and the greatest antidote to fear is boldness.

EXERCISE – BEING BOLD

Think about a situation in your life where fear is standing in your way and answer the following questions.

1 What exactly do you fear?
. . . .
2 How would you need to change your thoughts so that you could THINK BOLDLY about this situation?
. . . .
3 How would you need to change your behaviour so that you could ACT BOLDLY?
. . . .

Boldness releases powerful forces into the universe. Whenever we act boldly, and give it all we've got, our bodies go into a state of emergency and unlock many underused powers that we all possess, including energy, creativity, strength, stamina, endurance, flexibility and commitment.

- FACE YOUR FEAR
- THINK BOLDLY
- ACT BOLDLY
- FEEL AMAZING

Touch your soul

8   Touch Your Soul

A happy family, a meaningful career, enough money, good health, all these things are important and enhance the quality of our lives ... but they are not enough to create complete fulfilment. Someone I know is living through the last stages of cancer and each time I see her she seems more and more at peace with herself. Another friend has inherited a large amount of money and yet she often feels very depressed. When we look at our lives we are often tempted to think that *if only this would happen or I could meet that sort of person or if something would change, then I could be really happy*. What price is peace? Where can we find it? It is certainly not outside of ourselves and no one can bring it to us.

Peace, contentment, fulfilment and harmony are felt by the spiritual part of our being. Soul food cannot be bought at the supermarket. If the words 'spiritual' and 'soul' mean very little to you, think about a time when you felt 'touched' by something greater than yourself, when the world became a shining place for a moment. Let's touch that shining essence again.

EXERCISE – FINDING THE SOUL'S BREATH

1 Sit in a comfortable and relaxed position in a quiet place. Close your eyes and relax.
2 Put your right hand over your heart and say to yourself, 'I breathe the soul's breath.'
3 Exhale and wait until your breath comes in by itself. Pause briefly as your breath reaches its fullness and then let it go.

4 Wait until your breath naturally comes to fill the space; as you do this you will feel that the breath is coming to you rather than that you are doing something.

5 When your breath is coming to you in this way you are consciously breathing the soul's breath. As you breathe in this way continue to say to yourself, 'I breathe the soul's breath.'

When you do this exercise you will feel fabulous! What else is there to say?

Accept a compliment

9   Accept a Compliment

I take a lot of trouble to look nice for a party.

You   'Oh, you look lovely in that dress, is it new?'

Me   'What, this old thing? I've had it ages – I bought it in the sale.'

I spend a lot of time and effort on writing a report.

You   'This is a brilliant piece of work, you have obviously put a lot of time and effort into it.'

Me   'Oh, it was nothing.'

I cook a special meal.

You   'This meal is delicious. You really are a good cook.'

Me   'Oh, I'm not really, I just threw a few things together.'

Why do we find it so hard to accept a compliment gracefully? How do you feel when someone pays you a compliment? Perhaps you don't believe them. Do you make throwaway comments that spoil the effect of the compliment? We all do this in our embarrassment, and the result is that we belittle the compliment and devalue the opinion of the person giving it. How do you feel if you compliment someone and they don't accept it? Would you bother to do it again?

Whenever someone congratulates, encourages and supports you they are showing you respect and admiration. If you 'throw away' their compliment you are only showing your lack of self-esteem.

Learn to accept a compliment. The next time someone

says something nice about you just say 'thank you'. It might be difficult at first but keep on trying. Accept a compliment and you will feel wonderful and so will the person giving it.

Finish an uncompleted job

10 Finish an Uncompleted Job

How many unfinished jumpers are there in your cupboard? Unfinished books on your shelf? Partly written letters in your bureau? Unused jam recipes in your larder? How many of your inspirations have only partly materialized? Sometimes it doesn't matter if the project is unfinished, maybe it wasn't what you thought it would be. If that half jumper is a disaster then throw it away. We all have half-completed jobs that we don't finish which we continually think we 'should' finish. These unfinished projects are wind-ups – either throw them out and forget about them or finish them.

EXERCISE

1 Make a list of all your unfinished jobs.

_____

_____

_____

2 Decide which ones can hit the rubbish bin.
3 Choose one of the rest and FINISH IT! Your self-respect will reach dizzy heights.

Celebrate your aloneness

11 Celebrate Your Aloneness

You are unique. There is no such thing as a normal or average size or type of person. Everyone is absolutely special and individual. When we recognize our uniqueness we also recognize our aloneness. Sometimes our aloneness can be very scary. We may feel lonely because no one can ever really understand how we feel and always 'be there' for us. It is true that no one will ever know the inner you. You are the only person who can know yourself. No one else can be inside you. And would you really want anyone to know everything about you?

This idea of our aloneness also carries a wonderful quality of freedom. We can release our expectations of other people to know all about us and we can stop feeling guilty about not always 'being there' for others.

Frightening or freeing – your aloneness can be either of these things. Choose freedom, choose to celebrate your aloneness. Repeat the following affirmation which will help you to accept and enjoy the inevitability of feeling alone.

AFFIRMATION: *I am sitting on top of the world and I belong to nobody and nobody belongs to me.*

As you say this affirmation use your imagination and visualize yourself at the top of the world feeling free.

Feel the freedom which comes with these words. When we are truly free to be ourselves all our relationships improve and we feel wonderful.

Re-invent yourself

12 Re-invent Yourself

One of the fantastic things about going on holiday is that because no one knows you, you can feel free to be different.

We can easily become reflections of what people expect of us and these expectations can lead us into staying the same: wearing the same clothes, looking the same, doing the same things, saying the same things. For example, if your image is neat, quiet and respectable, it's difficult to suddenly decide to go a bit wild. Our friends and loved ones get alarmed when we behave out of character and so, if it gets too uncomfortable to make a change, we just slip back into our usual image.

I used to live in a small village where everyone knew everyone else. When I went to a big city I had a wonderful experience of anonymity – I felt free to be and do anything and I often discovered new things about myself in that sort of environment. However we don't have to drastically change our surroundings or go on holiday to be free to be different. We can re-invent ourselves. I have a friend who is always changing. One day she will wear a suit and the next day she will appear in loose hippy-style clothing. She is always changing her hair colour and style and embarking on new hobbies and interests. She says that she likes to keep changing her image so that she keeps herself on her toes and keeps interested in her life. When we are feeling flat we usually fall into an easy habitual lifestyle, where we do what we always do. This might give temporary security but it does not give a buzz to our lives. Recharge your life by changing something about yourself – dare to be different.

EXERCISE – BEING DIFFERENT

Do something which is out of character. Here are a few ideas.

1 Change your style of dress.
2 How long have you had the same hairstyle? More than a year? Change it.
3 Find a new friend, someone who is quite unlike you.
4 Start a new hobby or join a nightclass.
5 Change your makeup/aftershave.
6 Do you always wear dark colours? Put on some bright clothes and feel the difference.
7 Visit a different restaurant.
8 Go to a different pub.

Begin with small changes and notice how you feel. If being different is difficult at first, just keep on practising. Change is like a breath of fresh air, enjoy the new perspectives it brings.

Use your anger

13 Use Your Anger

Act out of your anger and not in it. Remember the last time that you were really angry? How did you act? Did you behave assertively and resolve your anger or did you just see red and say and do all the wrong things? In other words, did you act *out* of your anger or did you act *in* it?

Often we seem to become angry for the most trivial reasons. Can you remember a situation when you became explosively angry over what seemed to be an unimportant incident? How did you feel after this outburst? When we 'let rip' in this way it's easy to feel guilty and foolish and then to feel *even more angry* because we are angry with ourselves for behaving in this way. We can use or abuse the powerful energy of our anger.

EXERCISE – A VOLCANO OF ANGER

We are often afraid of our anger – it is a powerful force. So, when the sparks are about to fly we can become confused by a mixture of emotions, including resentment, hatred, guilt and fear. The next time this happens try the following four steps.

1 Accept your anger and allow yourself to *feel* it.
2 Recognize that this is your own powerful energy.
3 Visualize a volcano going off inside you, filling you with power and energy. Have the major eruption inside of you rather than outside. In this way you can consciously use your anger rather than letting your anger use you.
4 This initial inner blast will clear your mind so that you can act and speak coherently and assertively.

Releasing your inner volcano might even leave you feeling that there is nothing left to say. We often 'let rip' at the wrong person when we have accumulated a lot of anger. When you have cooled out, search for the real source of your anger, then communicate your feelings to the right person.

Anger is a natural emotion which only becomes dangerous if we continue to deny it. Act *out of your anger* (using your power constructively) rather than *in your anger* (going berserk) and there will be a dramatic change in the way that you feel.

Take a shower of light

14 Take a Shower of Light

Whenever you need a lift, whether it is to energize yourself or to 'throw light' on a problem, try taking a shower of light. You can do this at any time, in any place, and no one will be any the wiser.

VISUALIZATION

Imagine that you are standing under a shower. See large drops of white light falling over you and enveloping you. Feel the light as it embraces you. See the white light turn into the colours of the rainbow. Immerse yourself in the colours. Choose any colour which you feel drawn to (this is the colour that you need right now) and spend a few moments bathing in this coloured light. Feel and absorb this colour. Be aware of the properties of this colour entering your mind, body and spirit. If another colour comes to mind, repeat the process. Take all the colours that you need. When you are ready, mentally turn off the shower.

The shower of light is a spiritual cleansing of your whole being. Do it anywhere, it only takes a moment. Put your co-workers in a shower of white light and see the difference in your working day! The shower of light is a wonderful experience both to have and to give. Just try it.

Consciously change your environment every day

15 Consciously Change Your Environment Every Day

Research shows the more that we feel able to express ourselves in our environment the more relaxed and happy we are able to become.

Every day do something to make your surroundings more beautiful.

Examples
- Put fresh flowers in your bedroom.
- Bring a photo for your desk at work.
- Change a room around.
- Wash the curtains.
- Put a plant in your office.
- Move the pictures around in your house.
- Play beautiful music while you do the housework.
- Light a candle when you sit down for a meal.

The vibrations in your environment affect your well-being. Keep them bright and positive at home and at work. Give your surroundings some Tender Loving Care and feel the difference.

Praise a child

16 Praise a Child

When we recognize children in a positive way we are helping them to develop good, positive emotional and behaviour patterns, and we are developing their self-esteem. Using praise is one of the most powerful ways of allowing a child to feel good about herself. When we say things like, *'You did well, very good, I'm proud of you,'* we can feel the warm glow in the child's heart and we have a warm glow in our heart too. When we give positive support we feel great ourselves (all the more reason to give it!).

We can produce amazing results by taking *general praise* one step further and adding *descriptive praise*. This means noticing and mentioning specifically what it is that the child is doing well. Sometimes we may find ourselves saying to our children, *'Oh yes, that's marvellous, great, brilliant,'* without really paying too much attention. This sort of praise can lose it meaning if we are not careful. To make our praise even more effective we need to slow down and really pay attention to what the child is doing. Then we can also give specific information about *what they actually did* that was so great.

Examples

Praise   You are brilliant!
Descriptive praise   You kept on trying and you worked out how to do it all on your own.
Praise   What a lovely piece of writing!
Descriptive praise   The ideas you used are really original and your handwriting is so neat.

So you can praise the child, 'You are brilliant,' and then add why they are brilliant. 'You kept on trying and you worked out how to do it on your own'. This descriptive feedback gives the child an extra boost.

There is nothing quite like the feeling you get when you encourage a child to feel good about herself – everyone gets a warm glow! If you haven't got a child, go out and find one to appreciate! Praise a niece, a nephew, a next-door neighbour – they will feel great and so will you!

Laugh yourself silly

17 Laugh Yourself Silly

How do you feel when you have had a really good laugh?
You feel great, don't you? Laughing and smiling actually
have amazing health-giving effects.

- As you laugh you exercise your belly area and
  diaphragm.
- This abdominal movement deepens your breathing,
  which increases the oxygen flow into your body and
  improves your circulation.
- Laughing expands blood vessels, which encourages
  tissue healing.
- Smiling and laughing stimulates the production of
  endorphins (your body's natural painkillers), which
  produce a natural high.
- When you laugh you are helping your lymphatic system
  to get rid of bodily wastes, you burn off fat and relax
  your muscles.
- 'Laughter is the best medicine.' You can't have a really
  good laugh and be anxious and stressed at the same time.
- When you see the funny side of life you are more able to
  put things in perspective. It's easier to ask yourself if
  your problem really matters that much.

What incredible benefits! However fed up you feel it surely
is worth trying to find something to laugh about. Start with
a smile; a smile can start to change your mood. Seek out
something that has made you laugh in the past – a video, a
book, the company of a certain friend, an activity …

Put a smile on your face and go for laughter, it can only
make you feel 100 per cent better.

Clean your aura

18 Clean Your Aura

Have you ever met anyone and immediately felt the strength of their presence and personal power? We call this human quality 'personal magnetism', and indeed that is exactly what it is. Surrounding our physical body is a protective electro-magnetic field which is composed of our own radiations. We call this energy field the 'aura' and it can be seen by some people as a halo of light. Most of us don't 'see' the aura but we can 'feel' it by being aware of it. Maybe you are aware of a greyness around a person who has just smoked a cigarette or a brightness around someone who is being positive. Our auras are absorbers of energy and soak up vibrations from *everything* around us – the sun, moon, animals, plants, stones, people … We need to be aware of our auras, to keep them strong and intact and clear so that we can maintain good health and strong positive energy.

VISUALIZATION

Sit comfortably, close your eyes, steady your breathing and relax. Be aware of the energy surrounding your body. Imagine a halo of light surrounding your entire body, following the contours of your body from the top of your head down one side and back up the other side of your body to your head again. Follow this contour in your mind, visualizing an unbroken line of light surrounding your whole body. If you become aware of any weak points as you do this, consciously strengthen your aura in these places. Now send a white beam of cleansing light around the contour of your aura. Imagine this light as a vacuum cleaner sucking out any dirt and negativity. When your aura looks bright and clean open your eyes. With your freshly cleansed aura you will feel like a million dollars. Clean your aura regularly and maintain your positive energy.

Achieve your goals

19 Achieve Your Goals

Someone once said that if you get in a car and don't know where you are going you will drive around until you run out of petrol and never get there. If we have no goal how can we ever achieve anything? To lead a rich and full life we need to be able to mark our successes. It's all too easy to work hard towards something and then, as we find ourselves coming close to our achievement, to subtly move the goal posts and so ensure that we never actually score the goal. Have you ever done this? People who are only satisfied by perfection move their goal posts all the time and often find it hard to finish a project (it never seems to be quite good enough). Forget about being 'good enough': let go of your very high standards and make you goals realistic, achievable and rewardable.

EXERCISE – ACHIEVING MY GOALS

1 Specify three short-term goals (achievable within three months).
* . . . .
* . . . .
* . . . .
2 Write down exactly what you will need to do to achieve each one.
* . . . .
* . . . .
* . . . .
3 Focus on these goals and the action you will need to take to achieve them. Work towards the goals and don't change them as you get close to completion (no moving goal posts).

4 Allow yourself to achieve your goal (however modest you think it is). And then mark the achievement with a reward to yourself (make this real).

The successful completion of short-term goals leads inevitably to the achievement of long-term goals as we gain confidence in our ability to make things happen. Make your goals real (write them down). Give yourself a time limit (deadlines can be great motivators). Reward yourself with a real prize. You will feel brilliant.

Forgive your parents

20 Forgive Your Parents

Family get-togethers are not always the intimate and close gatherings that we would like them to be. Do you remember a Christmas when tempers ran high?

If you have a wonderful understanding relationship with your parents then this will not seem relevant to you. However, most of us, at some time, feel the need to clear up our relationship with our parents. Perhaps your mother sometimes still treats you like a child, maybe it is very difficult to have a close emotional relationship with your father. Whatever your personal family difficulties, there is one area that all of us need to 'clear up': we all need to forgive our parents.

As we learn more about ourselves we understand the way that negative patterning is passed on from parent to child. There comes a time when we start to recognize that many of our self-limiting beliefs were learned from our parents and from our childhood environment. We may then feel angry with our parents, thinking such things as: *'Why did my mother treat me like this? Why didn't my father show me that he loved me? Why did he hit me? Why did she let him treat me badly? Why did they always laugh at me? Why did they say I was stupid? Look how it ruined my confidence …'*

We can all find ways to blame our parents, and we will. Our children find ways to blame us, and they do.

Remember, your parents did the best they could. We can only teach and pass on what we already know, and that is what they did. You may have recognized some of your own negative behaviours, thoughts and feelings in your parents. As soon as you recognize this patterning you are beginning a big change in your life. You cannot let go of negativity and

39

replace it with positivity if you are still blaming your parents. Let go of whatever you think your parents 'did' to you. Talk about these issues to a counsellor if you think you need professional help. Start to forgive your parents and you will start to feel like a new person. This process may take a while, but every time you forgive a bit more you will feel lighter and brighter.

Remember, your parents had parents too!

Reframe your situation

21 Reframe Your Situation

This might be hard to believe, but nothing is actually stressful in itself. *Stress lies in the eye of the beholder*. In other words, if you see a person, situation or event as threatening, your mind, body, spirit and emotions will register stress.

EXERCISE – REFRAMING YOUR SITUATION

1 Think of a personal situation which is a problem for you right now. It could be to do with a relationship, work, family … choose something which is causing you worry and tension.
2 Find a quiet place, relax, close your eyes and visualize the problem in glorious Technicolor©. Now, take the person/event/situation and drain all the colour out of the picture.
3 Imagine the image getting smaller and smaller, shrinking until it has disappeared.
4 Now create a big, bold and colourful picture of you dealing brilliantly with the situation. See yourself looking confident, finding a resolution to the problem and feel your success.

Use this technique to change any negative aspects of your life –

• See the image.
• Drain the colour.
• Shrink the picture.
• See and feel a bright new positive image.

Reframe your negative pictures and take the stress out of your life.

Receive an angelic blessing

22 Receive an Angelic Blessing

EXERCISE – MAKE A SET OF ANGELIC BLESSING CARDS

Transfer the words below on to paper or card, to make your own set of 30 Angelic Blessing Cards. These cards provide key words that will help you to focus on particular aspects of your inner life.

SIMPLICITY
FLEXIBILITY
SPONTANEITY
ADVENTURE
HUMOUR
TRUTH
BEAUTY
COMPASSION
FAITH
LOVE

ENTHUSIASM
SURRENDER
INSPIRATION
GRATITUDE
COURAGE
WILLINGNESS
HARMONY
FORGIVENESS
UNDERSTANDING
INTEGRITY

HEALING
GRACE
HONESTY
RESPONSIBILITY
OPENNESS
CLARITY
CREATIVITY
TENDERNESS
FREEDOM
BALANCE

Find a quiet place and lay out your cards face down in front of you. Relax and close your eyes and then turn your attention to a particular problem for which you need help. Silently ask for divine assistance and as you do you will feel your energy changing. When you are ready, choose a card. The card you choose is the Angelic essence which you need to absorb at this time. Close your eyes again and absorb the qualities that this card brings. The Angel who represents this essence will be with you as you go about your business (I often take an Angel to work with me in my pocket). Think about the quality reflected by the card and as you do you will find this quality reflecting in all manner of ways throughout your day. Ask for an Angelic blessing and choose a card whenever you feel the need. Strengthen your divine connection and amazing things will happen.

Believe that you deserve the best

23 Believe That You Deserve the Best

I have met many people who have been using positive affirmations and creative visualization techniques who say that they have reached a point when they feel 'stuck' and that the affirmations just don't seem to be working any more. If this happens to you, always look at your beliefs about deservability. If you don't believe that you deserve the best then you will not allow good things into your life.

EXERCISE – DESERVING

1 What do you deserve?

_____

_____

Do you think that you deserve to fulfil your dreams?
Do you deserve the best that life has to offer?
Do you believe that you don't deserve very much or, in fact, that you deserve nothing at all?
2 Why are you a deserving person?
        or
  Why are you not a deserving person?
Answer whichever question you think applies to you.

_____

_____

Examine closely your beliefs about what you think you deserve. Where have these beliefs come from? What did your parents say about what you deserved? Did you deserve a clip around the ear or a good telling-off? What did your parents think that they deserved? Did they feel that they deserved the good things in life? Perhaps they were disappointed by life; maybe they felt that they didn't get what they deserved. Think about all the 'deserving' messages you may have received, whether spoken to you or picked up in more subtle ways.

AFFIRMATION: *I deserve the best in life.*

Repeat this affirmation over and over. Say it in the car, sing it in the shower, look in the mirror and say it. Say it enough times and it will start to take the place of any non-deserving messages you may have circling around your mind. Believe that you deserve the best and you will get it!

Accentuate the positive, eliminate the negative

24 Accentuate the Positive, Eliminate the Negative

Thoughts are powerful things; whatever you put your attention to will grow. Imagine that your mind is a garden. You can fill your mind with beautiful flowers or let it become overgrown and out of control with weeds. We can't have two opposing thoughts at the same time, so if you're holding a positive thought then there is no room for a negative thought. Actively plant positive seeds in the garden of your mind and weed out any negatives as soon as they appear. As soon as you are aware of a negative entering your mind, nip it in the bud. Then think of its opposite and form a good strong positive mental picture; let this replace the negative. It may take a while to recognize your negatives (they come in many disguises and you have been comfortable with them all your life). As you actively plant positive seeds in your mind you will find it easier to recognize the negative intruders.

EXERCISE – REPLACING NEGATIVES

- If you feel angry think the biggest loving thought that you can. There's not room for both thoughts.
- If you feel rushed, stop, close your eyes and visualize a beautiful calm scene.
- If you feel like a loser repeat the affirmation, '*I am a winner.*'

When we can fill our minds with beautiful thoughts our world becomes a beautiful place.

Remember: be here now

25 Remember: Be Here Now

It's Saturday morning, a day off, time to go shopping. As you get in the car one of the children starts complaining. 'Be quiet we must go shopping.' Then the baby cries, you are getting uptight. Your partner starts yelling. 'Oh stop yelling, he's only a baby.' Things are getting very tense … STOP! Do you recognize this sort of scene? Substitute any situation where your well-formed plans aren't working. Don't keep bashing on in the face of such resistance … stop and recognize the moment. Consciously place yourself into the present moment. Let go of thoughts about the past or the future and appreciate and act in the NOW.

If you get so organized and together that you are busy living in the future or you are rushing to keep track of time then you are missing the true pleasure of the moment. Whenever you feel that your life is running out of control, stop and say to yourself, *'Remember, be here now!'* This doesn't mean that you have to let go of everything. Sort out the babies and *then* go shopping. If the telephone rings then answer it (it's happening in the moment). Make that appointment for three weeks' time (you make it in the moment and in three weeks' time you will keep the appointment in the moment).

The power is always in the moment. Stop reading and recognize the moment, *feel the now*. 'Later' never actually exists because we are only ever really conscious in the present moment and 'later' always lies in the future.

The following affirmation will help you to stay in the present and to appreciate this precious moment of your life.

AFFIRMATION: *I accept the here and now fully as it is, right at this moment.*

Identify and eliminate unnecessary stressors

26 Identify and Eliminate Unnecessary Stressors

A certain amount of stress encourages us to achieve and to be dynamic in our lives as we learn to overcome life's challenges. However, too much stress can cause exhaustion, depression, lethargy and even illness. We all react differently to situations. On person's stress exhilarator (yes I *can* meet that deadline) is another's stress poison (no I'll never do it, it's all too much for me). Identify the unnecessary harmful stress in your life and eliminate it.

EXERCISE

Make a list of all the things that are negatively stressful to you. Think carefully about each stressor. Can you let go of it, change it or accept it in some way? Make a table like the one shown on page 52 and find a constructive approach to the elimination of unnecessary stress in your life.

Stressor	Let go	Change	Accept	Consequences
I always feel lethargic.		Cut down on alcohol and junk food. Eat healthily and take more exercise.		Feeling better. Looking better. Feeling more in control. Increased self-respect.
I'm always looking for a man/woman to make my life complete.	Do without an intimate relationship for a while. Learn to get to know myself.			Increased self-esteem. I know that I am an interesting person and I don't have to depend on others for acceptance.
I hate ……… (name of person)			Forgive, accept and release this person from your angry thoughts.	Feeling of lightness and freedom as I release my anger and hatred. Increased self-respect.

Spice up your life

27 Spice up Your Life

Here is a fantastic technique which is practical and mind-expanding at the same time. You can do it anywhere and create an amazing experience for yourself. It's called 'self-remembering' and introduces the concept of the 'witness'. How many 'yous' are there inside you? By lunchtime today I have been: happy/hungry/angry/thoughtful/serious/annoyed/tired/energetic/humorous.

How many 'yous' have you been today? We play many parts throughout our day and who 'you' are changes at every moment. We can often let ourselves off the hook by lessening the power we give to these passing 'you' states. Sometimes one 'you' does something for which every other 'you' must pay, maybe for the rest of your life. Our 'yous' are numerous and are all evaluative and judgmental. Can you remember doing something for which you cannot forgive yourself?

When you use self-remembering you adopt the role of witness as you go about your everyday life. The witness observes all your doings *but does not judge your actions in any way*. For example, you may eat a cream cake and then get annoyed with yourself for eating it. However, the witness would dispassionately note:

1 She is eating a cream cake
2 She is annoyed with herself for eating a cream cake.

If it feels hard to observe yourself in this way just imagine that you are standing outside of your body watching yourself (don't spend time analysing this method, just do it). At first you will probably only remember to witness when you are feeling calm and uninvolved – it is easy to forget when you get hooked by your emotions.

Cultivate your witness and experience something quite different in your life. Calm self-observation displaces angry self-criticism and ordinary events take on a different dimension. Practising witnessing, forgetting to witness and then remembering again can be great fun. It is an entirely private affair and it adds spice to the most mundane of tasks. Take your witness to the supermarket and have an ecstatic shopping experience!

Use your time happily

28 Use Your Time Happily

Are you managing your time effectively and happily? Are you able to make time for the things you love to do?

EXERCISE

1 Look at how you use your time. Draw a circle about six inches in diameter. Think about the way your time is used in different activities and divide up your 'pie'. This is your 'time use' pie chart.

TIME USE   FULFILMENT GAINED

2 Now put this chart aside. Using another piece of paper draw another circle to represent those activities where you gain most fulfilment. Don't look at the first chart while you are drawing the second one.
3 Put the charts side by side.

- What are the differences between the two?
- How could you manage your time to allow for more personal satisfaction?
- When you do this could you face any difficulties?
- How can you deal with these potential difficulties?

Replace 'should' with 'could'

29 Replace 'Should' with 'Could'

Write down all the things that you think you should do.

I should ....
....
....

Give yourself a time limit here or you could be at it for hours.

Examples
- I should read a lot more.
- I should love my mother.
- I should be more positive.
- I should be nicer to people.
- I should lose weight.
- I should get up earlier in the morning.

Now, take each 'I should' from your list, read it out loud and then ask yourself, 'Why should I?' Speaking out loud to yourself in this way makes the technique more effective. Voicing your feelings can help your understanding. Write down your answers. You may be surprised by what you have written.

Examples
- Because people won't like me any more.
- My father said I should.
- What will happen to me if I don't?
- Because everybody has to.
- Because I'm too lazy/stupid/worthless/careless ... etc.

The answers to 'Why should I?' questions show us how we can limit ourselves by holding certain beliefs. Try ending an 'I should' statement with 'because I really want to'. The sentence doesn't make sense because the word 'should' implies reluctance. Its use also indicates feelings of guilt and fear. Do we really need to burden ourselves in this way? Whenever you think or say that you 'should' or 'ought' to do something, recognize that you are putting yourself in the wrong in some way. Change your list, replacing 'should' with 'could' and start each statement with, 'If I really wanted to'.

Examples
• If I really wanted to I could read a lot more.

Rewrite your list in this way and you might find that there are some things that you don't even want to change! Don't be a 'should' victim, trapped by guilt. Allow yourself the possibility of 'could' and you will become free to allow positive changes into your life.

Make a success list

30 Make a Success List

When we are feeling low in self-esteem it is difficult to like anything about ourselves. When we are caught in a negative spiral of:

self-dislike ➜ feelings of powerlessness ➜ inability to make decisions ➜ inability to act ➜ self-dislike.

There is a way to stop the rot. People who come for counselling often say how much they hate themselves. If I ask them to tell me about any positive things that they have experienced in their lives they find it very difficult to begin. One way to lift ourselves out of this negative cycle is to think about what we have done well in the past. *Maybe things don't look so good now, but what sort of achievements have we already made in our lives?* I ask people to make a 'success list'. This is a list of *everything* you are successful at, or have been a success at, or done successfully at some time in your life. Include all areas of your life: relationships, work, leisure. Write down everything that is meaningful to you, even if it might not be to someone else. Your list may start small, but the more you think about it the more you will remember your accomplishments. What about coming first in the sack race on Sports Day? Do you remember learning to ride a bike? You will certainly remember having a baby! How about getting your first job? Going on your first date. Starting school. Passing your driving test. Go back as far as you can, make a fun thing of it, get a really big piece of paper and keep adding to the list. Memories of success will change your mood. Look at your list, what an incredible set of experiences! You see, you aren't powerless, helpless and indecisive after all – you are a SUCCESS!

Choose the colours you need

31 Choose the Colours You Need

We all respond to colour, and scientists have discovered that each colour sends a unique message to the brain which affect our moods in different ways. Look at the chart below and think about how your own clothes and decor can enhance particular moods.

Red   Represents the body and is physically stimulating. Wear it for energy. Red can encourage confrontation in others (so take care).

Yellow   Relates to your ego and your emotions. Good for increasing optimism and creative confidence.

Orange   Relates to sex. Orange increases warmth, physical enjoyment and security. Wear it to lift your love-life.

Green   Represents natural healing and balance. Wear green to restore your energies and inspire harmony in others.

Pink   Links with our feminine, nurturing qualities. Wear it to attract some TLC (tender loving care).

Blue   Corresponds to our intellectual side and is logical, calm and soothing. Good for when you want to appear cool or when you want to do some serious thinking.

Purple   Represents spiritual awareness. Good for when

you are looking inward and thinking of higher things.

Make conscious use of colour in your environment and when you choose your clothes, to bring out the best in yourself.

Increase your personal power

32 Increase Your Personal Power

When we are high in personal power we are:

- High in self-esteem
- Energetic and dynamic
- Effective
- Imaginative
- Purposeful
- Decisive
- Focused

How often do you feel like this? The concept of power is often linked with ideas of struggle, authority and conflict. We are using the word quite differently here. Your power is your own. It belongs to you and no one can change it, take it away or give you more. You create your own personal power or not as the case may be. If we want to be high in personal power we have to take total responsibility for everything that happens to us in our life.

Whenever we start blaming external forces or other people for the things that happen to us, we give away our personal power.

Examples
After being give a poor seat in a restaurant: *'It's not fair, I never get given a good seat.'*

Working late for the third night in a row: *'My boss never thinks that I might have something better to do.'*

Whenever we wait for someone to change their behaviour we are giving away our power.

Example
'He doesn't mean to ignore me, he just has a problem showing his true feelings. I will change him!' (Many women will recognize this one).

If you are waiting for someone to change you will wait forever. Every time you play the victim you give away your power to your victimizer. If it's someone else's fault then you can't do anything to change your situation. Take charge of your life: say 'no' when you need to, express your true feelings and don't let people treat you like a doormat. Let go of blame, increase your personal power and be free to live your life dynamically.

Soften your focus

33 Soften Your Focus

This world is a wonderful place.

How do you respond to this statement? We often let our
lives become humdrum and ordinary. As the years pass we
are inclined to live our lives more and more according to
our habits. Perhaps you always go through the same ritual
when you get up in the morning, and such a habit may be
useful because it saves time. However, habitual responses
in our thought, behaviour and emotional processes can
limit our experiences and take the magic and spontaneity
from our lives. Here is a technique to help you to lift out of
your habitual behaviour into a state of alert and enhanced
awareness:

EXERCISE – SOFTENING YOUR FOCUS

1 Next time you are walking down the street stare at the pavement or look
  ahead and become aware of the focus of your vision. How far are you
  looking?
2 Now stop and expand your awareness. Rather than focus on one thing,
  expand your visual awareness; you will feel your focus 'softening' as you
  do this.
3 Become conscious of all those things in the corners of your vision,
  experience the colours and shapes of everything in your newly softened
  and enlarged focus.
4 Practise for a while and soon you will automatically begin to experience
  your environment in new ways. Extend and soften your focus in a social
  situation – you will be surprised at the additional information you will
  pick up about other people.

Your life will lose its 'ordinariness' as you soften your focus and take in more about your environment. Look for more and you will experience more! Keep practising.

Make your own mission statement

34 Make Your Own Mission Statement

Writing and developing a personal mission statement cannot happen instantly because it requires you to think about yourself in an entirely new way. Ask yourself these questions:

1 What is it that you believe that you do, that makes a difference to people and to mankind?
2 What motivates you to do the things that you think are important?
3 Why do you do the things you do?

These questions will be difficult to answer until you realize that you, personally, can make an amazing impact on this world. What special strengths do you bring that can help to make positive changes in your relationships and in your immediate environment?

List your strengths.

• ....
• ....
• ....

Well, what is your mission statement? In other words, what is your life's purpose, why exactly are you here? To raise consciousness about environmental issues? To make the world a happier place? To ensure that your children have high self-esteem? To raise money for a worthwhile cause? To make people laugh? To teach? To listen to others?

When you can make a mission statement (or more than one) your life will have new direction and purpose. Remember that you bring your own unique set of skills and strengths to this planet and you came to use those abilities.

Discover what drives you from within and match it with real-world activities to give your life new meaning.

Have a think slim, be slim day

35 Have a Think Slim, Be Slim Day

You know those days when you wake up feeling lethargic, bloated and overfed and low in the attraction stakes. Get a grip on your day and turn it into a 24-hour programme which will take off a little weight, make you feel spiritually lighter, more in control and will increase your feelings of self-respect.

THE PLAN FOR THE DAY

Morning: Take a shower (as cold as you can bear) to wake you up and get your circulation going. Put on comfortable clothes which are in bright invigorating colours (red and oranges if you have them). Sip hot water with a squeeze of lemon – this will help to clear out the accumulated toxins in your body. Be still and quiet, use one of the meditations in this book to calm your mind. Do some exercise. If you are used to aerobic exercise do something energetic, if not just do some simple stretches, or jog on the spot for a few minutes. By now your body will be feeling more in tune. Have a slow, relaxing breakfast, maybe some fruit and herb tea. Have a slice of wholemeal toast if you feel hungry (but no refined cereals). Keep your diet today as pure as you can. Remember to keep drinking the hot water and lemon every couple of hours (this will help to clear your system and sharpen your mind).

Afternoon: Choose a nutritious lunch which is low in calories but good for your body. Stay away from refined foods. Try homemade vegetable soup (steamed and blended vegetables) and a slice of wholemeal bread if you are at home. Follow this with a large glass of mineral water. (If you are at work, choose a light, wholesome sandwich and some fruit). When your lunch is digested have a 15-minute exercise boost. Repeat the morning exercise if you like. If you are at work, take a fast walk around the block in your lunch hour. Keep drinking your hot water and lemon.

Evening: Have a huge plateful of salad with some low-calorie protein (cottage cheese, boiled egg). Take time to prepare a really interesting salad and make it look attractive. Eat slowly (stay off the salad dressing, use a drop of cider vinegar with chopped herbs to add interest). Relax and listen to some restful music after dinner. Consider how well you approached your day and how well you have treated yourself. Take a 15-minute stroll and then relax in a warm bath before bed.

Tomorrow you will wake up feeling better and brighter and lighter.

Enjoy the music of the spheres

36 Enjoy the Music of the Spheres

We are busy people living in a busy world. Sometimes the demands of life can feel relentless as we rush around the universe doing this and doing that. When you feel caught on the treadmill of life … STOP and try this simple and wonderful meditation technique:

EXERCISE – CLIMBING THE LADDER OF SOUND

Get into a comfortable position where your head, neck and chest are in a straight line. You can lie down (as long as you don't fall asleep). Use earplugs if there is a lot of noise, but they aren't necessary if you can find a quiet time and place. Keep your mouth closed.

Now tune in to any inner sound that you can hear in your head. Home in on that sound until it is the main sound in your mind. Let all other sounds and thoughts pass by.

As you let this sound fill your consciousness you will ultimately merge with it until you can no longer hear it. At this point you will start to hear another sound. Now tune into this sound and repeat the process.

There are seven sounds, but it doesn't matter how many you think you hear because we all discriminate between sounds in a different way. The various descriptions of these sounds include: the song of the nightingale; the sound of cymbals; the ocean in a conch shell; the buzzing of bees; drumming and the sound of crowds in a large gathering place (such as a railway station). Listen for as long as you feel comfortable. Don't bother to try to define the sounds, just enjoy what is called 'the music of the spheres'.

Appreciate your team

37 Appreciate Your Team

Do you know who is in your team? Here I'm not referring to the local football team but to any group of people who work and co-operate with you. Teamwork and team-building are buzz words in the world of work because of course employers want people who can co-operate and communicate effectively with others. However, such important personal skills will enhance the performance of any group. You might belong to any number of teams: your work team, your family, parent group at school, darts club, sports club, drama group ... there are numerous possibilities. Make a list of all your teams.

My teams are:

....
....
....

Good teamwork involves commitment, shared goals, support for other members and good interpersonal skills. Being part of a team increases our sense of belonging and well-being and there is nothing quite like the shared feeling of a team achievement. Think about your own teams, increase your team effort and, above all, appreciate your own team members.

Stay forever young

38 Stay Forever Young

Children always want to 'grow up': to break their boundaries, to be allowed to do more and more, to stay up later, to be independent ... and then, suddenly, glorious adulthood is here. Free to do as we wish: to drink and smoke ourselves into a stupor, to eat junk food or not to eat, to have filthy bedrooms and wear dirty clothes. We can do whatever we like, at last we are free of parental restrictions, we are adults.

My youngest son longs to be a teenager and my teenage children are reminiscing over their childhood. But we can have both the freedom of adulthood and the joys of childhood if we remain young at heart. Fun people can be any age – staying young is an attitude, it has nothing to do with how old we are.

Get in touch with some of your childhood memories. We all have memories of sensual experiences which link us with our past. They may be smells, tastes, textures, noises, movements. Childhood memories can be rekindled by the touch of velvet; the taste of an acid drop; the smell of the sea; the sound of a church bell; a ride on a swing.

EXERCISE – REVISITING YOUR CHILDHOOD

Are there any sensual experiences which take you back to your childhood? Can you fill in any of the categories below?

TOUCH . . . .
TASTE . . . .
SMELL . . . .

If you have discovered any experiences which remind you of your childhood then *recreate that experience*. Go and eat a sherbet dip; look at the *Watch with Mother* video; ride a donkey; blow some bubbles; sit on a hay bale; go to the fair and smell the candy floss and even eat it ... Your list may start very small but as you pursue these memories you will open the floodgates of your childhood experiences. As you bite into that toffee apple you *are* the child within you. Allow your child inside to continue to play and to dance through life in a carefree way and you will stay forever young.

Make good vibrations

39 Make Good Vibrations

Your mind is a powerful energy broadcaster. Your thoughts are magnetic and they go out from you and draw to you those things that you think about. Think about how you feel when you spend time with someone who is extremely negative. The vibrations get very low and eventually affect your own mood. How do you feel when you spend time with someone who is positive and enthusiastic? The vibrations rise and you feel better for having met them. Your thoughts create your reality as they go out into the world and determine the events, people and objects which you attract into your life.

You can raise your energetic vibrations and feel lighter by using higher words and thoughts when you speak to yourself and to others. If you feel anxious or low use positive words to raise your energy. Say such words to yourself as: HARMONY, LOVE, PEACE, RADIANCE, BEAUTY, JOY, ENTHUSIASM, COMMITTED, DELIGHTFUL, INSPIRED … Think and speak of all the beautiful and inspiring words you know. Notice how, when you use these words when talking to other people, you will feel lighter and brighter. Use uplifting words in the company of others and watch and feel the changes in their energy and yours.

EXERCISE – HIGH WORDS, HIGH THOUGHTS, HIGH VIBRATIONS

This is a great exercise to do on the way to work. Take each letter of the alphabet and think of the highest word you can beginning with that letter. Use these words ABUNDANTLY and the effect will be AMAZING.

Search for the hero inside yourself

40 Search for the Hero Inside Yourself

Who do you most admire? Who are your own personal heroes and heroines? These people might be media celebrities, sports personalities or your friend up the road who is so good at keeping positive in spite of all her problems. Make a list of your heroes and write exactly why you admire them.

EXERCISE – MY HEROES AND WHY I ADMIRE THEM

1 ....
2 ....
3 ....

Now take one of your heroes and visualize him/her doing or being whatever it is that you most admire. Close your eyes and imagine walking right up to this person and stepping into their shoes. Imagine having the gifts and qualities that this person has. Let yourself 'be' this person for a few moments before you come back to yourself.

Look carefully at the qualities that you most admire in your list of people. And now think about yourself. At some level you already have these qualities. If you can recognize certain strengths in others then you must also be aware of the capacity for these in yourself (otherwise you would never have recognized them). You may never be a football star but you can always improve your game and become super-fit. You may never be a chat-show host but you can always improve your ability to talk effectively to others.

We humans are so much more than we think we are. However ordinary you imagine your life to be, you have in fact been given magical gifts. We take these gifts for granted, our abilities to share, to communicate, to understand: to care, to sympathize, to love, to transform, to create, to achieve ...

Search for the hero inside yourself who is able to use these gifts to create a full and incredible life.

Respect parenthood

41 Respect Parenthood

Parenthood is a hugely challenging area which can take us to heavenly heights and to hellish lows. As parents we are confronted with the popular cultural myths about parenting, fatherhood and motherhood. We do an amazing job in the face of a fundamental contradictory belief which is supported by the culture in which we live. Look at this confusing belief: *a mother has a powerful role/motherhood is not important*. So, if the hand that rocks the cradle rules the world, how come we mothers have so little status? No wonder we get confused.

EXERCISE – KEY POINTS TO REMEMBER ABOUT PARENTHOOD

Make a list of the following points and refer to it constantly. When the dinner is burning and the washing machine has broken down and you only had three hours sleep last night, remember YOU ARE NOT ALONE! Parents everywhere are doing a magnificent job; remind yourself to respect the act of parenthood. Put this list in a prominent place.

- Parenthood is a big job.
- I am a good parent. I am doing my best.
- Parenthood is vital – the survival of the race depends on it.
- Guilt is not an intrinsic part of parenthood. I don't *have* to feel guilty.
- When guilt engulfs me, I can just step out of it. Guilt ruins family life.
- I need to look after myself. I cannot give to others if I have nothing left to give.
- There are no perfect parents; we all make lots of mistakes. It's OK to make mistakes; this is how we learn.
- I am free to feel and to express all of my emotions.

- Parenthood is a state of potential conflict. I can accept this and work with it. I am flexible and creative.
- My children do what I do and not what I say.
- I forgive and thank my mother and father. They taught me what they knew about parenthood.
- It is safe for my children to grow up. I can easily let them go.
- I pass on my patterns of self-esteem to my children. I can create high self-esteem.
- I deserve a supportive and validating family life.

Take your day one step at a time

42 Take Your Day One Step at a Time

Not every day starts with a bang. Sometimes it's hard to find the energy to get up and out. You might have a lot on your mind; you may have a busy schedule; there may be difficulties to face. When your day gets off to a dreary start use the following technique.

TAKE ONE STEP AT A TIME

Concentrate on the immediate task in hand. Just get yourself out of bed before you think of the next job. *Take one step at a time.* Don't think about the next step until the immediate step is over. Each time you achieve one step, stop and congratulate yourself. (Well done Lynda, you managed to get to work). In this way every small task becomes an achievement, which indeed it is on a day when the going is rough. By refusing to be drawn into worrying about the rest of the day you protect yourself from negative thinking (*Oh how am I going to get to that meeting; pick up the children; do the shopping; cook the dinner; ... I'll never manage it all.*) As you achieve more and more tasks (congratulating yourself along the way) your view of the day will become much more positive and you will start to feel in control again. There is a fine feeling of accomplishment when we lift ourselves up in the face of adversity and one step at a time is the only way we can do it.

Do whatever turns you on

43 Do Whatever Turns You On

It is not necessary to take mood-enhancing/depressing drugs in order to change the way that we feel. Think of how easily your emotions can be changed by the simple things in life. Perhaps a certain piece of music can lift you, a walk, a piece of artwork, sex, a poem, surfing, driving, cooking, swimming, dancing, shopping, singing ... there is an infinite number of possibilities here. Start to notice what changes your mood for the better. Only very recently I discovered something which really turns me on. My new job required that I bought coloured paper, card, pens etc for creative projects with students. I realized, as I spent more and more time gazing at fluorescent card and board markers, that I really enjoy the buzz of a stationery store, with its goods offering such amazing potential for all sorts of creativity. Every time I went to buy stationery I would come away buzzing with new ideas. Now, I often just wander around the stationery departments in order to get this creative lift. We all get 'turned on' by very different things and they are very often the simple things in life.

EXERCISE – THE THINGS THAT TURN ME ON

Spend a couple of days really thinking about what it is that energizes and excites you. Then write your list.

- ....
- ....
- ....

Now do these things!

Look for the silver lining

44 Look for the Silver Lining

Life is full of ups and downs and we can learn from everything that happens to us. So, a relationship ends; we fail an exam; lose a job ... Once the initial anger/dependency/depression is over we can review our setbacks and use them to learn more about ourselves. Every event in our lives has a purpose, there is a powerful intention in every situation. Rather than remaining in a negative state which will only take you further down, try approaching the situation in a new way.

EXERCISE – FINDING THE SILVER LINING

Ask yourself the following questions:

- How did this happen?
- How can I see this situation differently?
- In what way can this loss work for me?
- What can I learn about myself here?
- What is there that is positive in this situation?

If this is hard to do, think back to a difficult time in the past. For example, you may have lost a job opportunity and so found yourself taking a totally different direction which turned out to be exactly 'right' for you. An intimate relationship may have ended leaving you heartbroken. Perhaps this relationship wasn't good for you and you only see this as your heart mends and you start to enjoy your new freedom and independence. As one door closes another opens. Look for the newly opening door, look for the silver lining.

Improve your sex life

45 Improve Your Sex Life

Physical attraction is always so strong at the beginning of a relationship. The tantalizing nature of the mating game, attracting and seducing, leaves the hormones in a perpetual state of excitement and the beloved is an amazingly erotic hero/heroine who can do no wrong. No wonder the sex is good! And then, if the fairytale comes true and we become a 'stable relationship', everything changes.

Increasing commitment and responsibility to each other bring peace and security. The early days of thrilling sexual excitement (Will he notice me? Will she ring? What a hero!) end. Things like jobs, children and mortgages inevitably affect our sex lives. Some people never have a permanent relationship because they can't bear to lose the thrill of the chase and the seduction. Others have affairs throughout their marriages for similar reasons. But it is possible to keep your sex life buzzing in a long-term (children/mortgage/jobs/shopping/drain-cleaning/putting out the rubbish) relationship.

Try the following.

- Focus your attention on your sex life. If it's losing its appeal, talk about it *to each other*.
- Keep talking about sex with each other (whenever it's possible). We can be sexual all day – we don't have to wait until we get into bed at night and turn off the light.
- Put the romance back into your relationship. Remember how it was at the start, recreate that atmosphere. Think about why you entered this relationship. What turned you on in the first place?

- Spend time alone with each other, turn off the television, stop cleaning the kitchen and enjoy each other.
- Laugh together. When we share humour we bring great intimacy into our relationship. A great sense of humour is a terrific turn-on!
- Change the way you do things, break some of your oh-so-comfortable/very boring routines. You will know what these are!
- Think about sex! This advice is for women. Research shows that men think about sex at least five times an hour (a very conservative estimate, I should think). Women often don't think about it at all! If you don't think about sex … start!

Stay cool

46 Stay Cool

Can you imagine how it would be to feel calm and centred as you go about your daily business? Some people say that they only feel truly alive when they are feeling strong and powerful emotions. But these heavy feelings lead us from a calm and balanced state onto a rollercoaster of emotional highs and lows. When we calm our emotions we don't stop having strong feelings, but they no longer rule our lives. We are more than a ragbag of emotions, we have a strong and powerful inner self which guides and directs us towards the good. If our emotions are turbulent we cannot connect with our wise inner self and then things start to get out of control.

Think of a time when your emotions ran away with you. Did you say what you wanted to say? Did you act the way you wanted to act? Did you get the result you wanted? The answers were most probably 'no'. It's hard to remain clear and in control when you are feeling hot and bothered. Here is a brilliant little exercise which will cool you out. Try it before you laugh at it. It really works!

EXERCISE – THE EMOTIONAL COOLER

If you are feeling worried, nervous, angry, upset or irritable try this:

1 Put your right thumb over your right nostril, just lightly closing it off.
2 Exhale. Inhale slowly through your left nostril only for twenty complete breaths.
   • Keep you mouth closed all the time
   • Make the breaths as long and smooth as you can

- Each time you exhale let go of all tension, hurt, anger, irritability and any other negative emotions. Visualize these emotions draining out of your body so that you feel clear and positive
3 You may have to excuse yourself for a few moments to do this (in the middle of a meeting for example). It's very useful during a heated telephone discussion and it is possible to do it without being detected (with careful thumb positioning).

Research has shown that physiological and psychological states are reflected in the way that we breathe. By controlling which nostril is functioning we can tune in to the different hemispheres of the brain. When we breath through our left nostril we are connecting with the right side of our brain, which controls our receptive, spiritual and inner awareness. Do this exercise now, before the heat is on, and feel the difference in your relaxation level.

Understand and increase your self-esteem

47 Understand and Increase Your Self-Esteem

On a bad day, when we are low in self-esteem and spiralling rapidly down into a pit of negativity, we see a world where everyone else is clever/getting it together/having amazing relationships/coping easily with stress … Of course the rest of the world is not really like this, it's just the way it seems when we feel out of control.

All human beings struggle with issues of self-esteem, yes even those oh-so-confident-looking folk. It seems as if our self-esteem is always on the line. We can go up and down and up and down again with alarming speed. (Does this sound like you?) Take heart, all of us are working on our self-esteem. We have to because we did not learn to believe in our intrinsic worthiness when we were children and so we need to learn it now. Our self-esteem is rather like a beautiful but delicate flower and it needs constant nourishment and care in order for it to grow and remain protected.

Use any of the tips in this book to pull yourself out of negativity and increase your good feelings about yourself. But before you do, take a moment to remember that whenever you are working on your self-esteem you are working on your own personal development. You are not alone, this job is a lifetime's work (and joy!). Don't get depressed about losing your self-esteem – it happens to all of us, all of the time. However, as you cultivate ways to bring positive changes into your life, your self-esteem will become more stable. Next time when you feel disheartened you will be able to pick yourself up quickly, dust yourself down and start all over again.

Discover your life's purpose

48 Discover Your Life's Purpose

You are the one and only you. Only you can make the contribution you came here to make. Your combination of special talents is unique and irreplaceable. You have come for a special purpose; to fulfil your life's work. Do you believe this to be true? Have you discovered your life's work? The feelings that come with fulfilling your life's purpose include: 'aliveness', energy, high self-esteem, harmony, interest, enjoyment and satisfaction. You will know if you are not doing your life's work because you will feel dissatisfied, incomplete, low in self-esteem, low in energy and generally out of sorts. These feelings indicate that you have wandered from your path. The following visualization is a powerful way to put yourself back on course.

VISUALIZATION – ATTRACTING YOUR LIFE'S WORK

Sit very quietly, relax and close your eyes. Imagine that your life's work can be represented by a symbol. Visualize what that symbol would be, take the first thing that comes to mind even if it seems inappropriate. Hold your symbol close to your body and feel its energy filling your whole being … Hold your symbol like this for a few moments … Sense the energy entering every cell of your body.

There is a hill ahead of you. Carry your symbol to the top of the hill. The journey is very easy for you to accomplish; your symbol is very light to carry. When you reach the top of the hill you see an arched gateway. As you stand under this archway you look behind and see, there below, everything that is a part of your life; all the hopes and fears, loves and disappointments, people and places – all the experiences it took for you to reach where you are today. You feel thankful for all your past experiences. The gateway leads to your future, and as you step through, you will throw your symbol high in the air and it will fly out into the world which is your future. Take a few moments to centre yourself before you step through this gateway. Look back at your past again if you wish to. Step through the gateway and release your symbol – this is your future.

This is a powerful visualization which will help you to attract all that you need to discover to fulfil your life's purpose. The concentrated energy which symbolizes your life's work is spinning through the universe and it is a strong magnet. This thought magnet will attract to itself the ways and means for you to find your true path and your true purpose in life. Follow your star and discover your life's work.

Just do it

49 Just Do It

What is it that you would most love to do but are afraid to do because of the consequences? The following exercise will help you to judge how realistic your fears actually are.

EXERCISE – AS GOOD AND AS BAD AS IT CAN BE

1 Name three things that you would love to do but that you are afraid to try.
   (a) ....
   (b) ....
   (c) ....

2 Ask yourself what would be the best and worst possible outcomes of doing each of these three things.

	BEST POSSIBLE OUTCOME	WORST POSSIBLE OUTCOME
(a)		
(b)		
(c)		

3 Ask yourself, 'What are my fears and anxieties?' and write them down.

4 Ask yourself, 'How realistic are these fears and anxieties?'
   Rate your score for realism on a scale of 1–10
   1 = TOTALLY UNREALISTIC   10 = TOTALLY REALISTIC

MY FEARS AND ANXIETIES REALISM SCORE

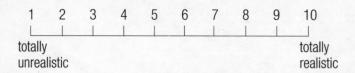

1 2 3 4 5 6 7 8 9 10

totally
unrealistic

totally
realistic

How realistic are your fears? If we long to do something and don't do it, that longing can last a lifetime. Usually our fears are irrational and groundless and our longing by far outweighs the reality of the fear. Go ahead – just do it! You will feel fantastic.

Treasure your valuables

50 Treasure Your Valuables

What is valuable to you? What do you most treasure in your life? We are not thinking about gold watches and diamonds here but rather things that you feel that you cannot do without. What is important to you in your emotional life? What feelings and people are important? What inspires you, makes you feel good, energizes you? Whatever makes you 'come alive' are your valuables: make a list of them.

My valuables are:

. . . .
. . . .
. . . .

Think about why you value these things. Why are they so precious to you? Take time to appreciate and treasure your valuables.

Expect a miracle

51 Expect a Miracle

A few years ago I was running a class for unemployed youngsters. I was going through the members of the group asking them what they thought they needed to help them to get a job and writing whatever they said next to their name. We had things like, more training, educational qualifications, better communication skills, computer knowledge ... And then I reached a young man who looked really together but was very low in self-confidence. He had made some mistakes in his early youth and had a police record. When I asked him what he needed to get a job he said, 'I need a miracle.' So next to his name I wrote 'needs a miracle' and everybody laughed. Then I wrote 'Believe in miracles' at the top of the board. The class left and the youth stayed behind. He was upset and he said, 'You know, I really do need a miracle.' I told him to go home and to start believing that miracles do happen. Within a week, through an incredible set of circumstances, he applied for a job that was advertised nationally. In the face of tough competition he got that job, left the class and we were all left speechless.

Miracles are love in action and if you don't believe in them they will never happen to you. We can attract miracles into our lives but only if we truly believe they are possible. Forget about not *really* allowing yourself to believe in case you are disappointed. Fear of disappointment will stand in your way for ever! You are disappointed anyway – what have you got to lose?

Expect a miracle for a week. Wholeheartedly believe that one will happen and keep trusting. The miracle might not be the one you were expecting but I can assure you that *something amazing* will happen. Belief is the most powerful magic of all.

Love your enemies

52 Love Your Enemies

This is such a powerful technique so please don't give up before you've given it a chance.

Make a list of all those people who you can't stand. If there's no one on your list, turn to the next page; however, I expect that you have some names. We all struggle with human relationships and unless we have achieved saintly perfection we will inevitably become irritated and angry with certain people in our lives.

There are two interesting issues here:

1 The things that we find most annoying in others are qualities which we are struggling with ourselves (that is why we are so irritated).
2 Life is a boomerang, whatever we send out we get back (in some way). Someone described the act of hating and resenting as being like 'hugging a poisonous snake to our bosom'. Feelings of ill-will fester and eventually erupt, often making us ill.

Choose someone from your list and reflect on these points. Ask yourself the following questions:

• Why *exactly* does this person irritate me so much? Look beneath the surface of your feelings. Does their behaviour mirror yours in any way?
• Is it worth making myself ill just so that I can go on hating them?

EXERCISE – LAST-DAY-ON-EARTH FORGIVENESS

When you next meet a person on your list imagine that it is their last day on earth and that you will never see them again. Take this chance to change the nature of your relationship.

Forgiveness is hard but possible. Forgiveness makes you feel FANTASTIC – it's worth all the hard work. The gifts it brings are the greatest we can receive.

Heal your life

53 Heal Your Life

'To heal' literally means 'to make whole' and every time we have a problem, whether it's mental, spiritual, emotional or physical, we are being shown a place where we need to heal ourselves (make ourselves whole). However good our doctor, psychotherapist, counsellor, osteopath, reflexologist, aromatherapist ... etc, we need to remember that ultimately our healing is in our own hands. Only we can choose to create health and balance in our lives.

However ill you feel, whatever psychological problems you face, you can still be in control of your own healing. If you have a physical condition find out all you can about it – don't just expect the doctor to 'sort you out'. Take the prescribed medicine but also investigate alternative approaches. Look at your lifestyle and nutrition – do they support good health? How about your relationships – are they supportive or stressful? Do you love your work or is it winding you up? Look beyond a single symptom, look at the *whole* picture of your life.

Do you need to change things to reduce undue stress and tension? If you do then that headache pill will never work, there are deeper issues here.

EXERCISE – HEALING YOURSELF

Love yourself
Forgive yourself.
Release all blame.
Release all negativity.

Express your needs.
Take care of your body.
Trust your intuition.
Develop your self-esteem.

Do these things and you will start to feel better and better and better!

Repeat the following affirmation throughout the day, whenever you remember. Sing it, say it, write it, shout it.

AFFIRMATION: *I deserve to be healthy.*

Take charge of your own healing and you will be back in control of your life.

Just face the music and dance

54 Just Face the Music and Dance

More important than *what* you do is *how* you do it. How do you do the things you do? Are you stumbling through life trying to cope with things that are 'happening' to you? Do you sometimes feel like a victim? Notice those people who seem to dance through life at their own tempo. Who do you know who is like this? These people, who are happy and successful, are living their lives at their own pace, they are refusing to be victimized and have made a positive decision to meet life 'head on'.

'Just face the music and dance' is such a wonderful phrase. It conjures up the image of risk-taking, decision-making, accepting challenges and making things happen in an entirely non-threatening way. Being assertive is not difficult. Maybe you will have to learn to say 'no' more often; you may have to put up with some people not liking you any more; others might become envious of you, but always remember, *whose life is this anyway?* Decide to stop playing the victim. Decide to be assertive. Face the challenges that life brings in a positive way and dance to your own tune.

EXERCISE – DANCING THROUGH YOUR PROBLEMS

Sit in a quiet place and thoroughly relax your body. Close your eyes and let your thoughts drift away. Now bring to mind all the problems that you have. See them in your mind's eye, see them crowding together, jostling for your attention. Now imagine yourself clearing a pathway between the crowds. Push the problems to the side and create a shining path which leads you to your future. Visualize yourself dancing along your path, recognizing your problems as you skip past but not letting them stand in your way. If it is difficult to create this image think of Dorothy dancing along the Yellow Brick Road.

When you are feeling great about yourself others are attracted to you. Positivity attracts positivity. Don't let your problems drag you down, dance lightly through your life. Dance and the world dances with you.

Calm your mind

55 Calm Your Mind

We know how to satisfy our material desires by going out into the world and experiencing things, feeling things and doing things. However, if we live our lives only at the material level we will eventually feel disenchanted. All the possessions, friends and abilities in the world do not compensate for a lack of spiritual connection. Don't forget that you are mind, body and spirit, and spiritual nourishment reaches the parts that nothing else can reach. Get in touch with your spirit and calm your mind and body with this simple technique.

EXERCISE

1 Find a quiet and peaceful place and sit in a comfortable chair so that your back remains straight.
2 Close your eyes and begin to watch your mind. Let your thoughts come and observe them. Don't get involved with your thoughts, just notice them.
3 When you are ready, turn your attention to your breathing. Notice the muscle in your abdomen, just below your rib cage, which rises and falls as you breathe. Follow its movement. Each time the muscle rises think, 'rising' and every time it falls, think 'falling'. Rising ... falling ... rising ... falling ... let all your other thoughts drift away as you focus on this muscle. At first your mind will keep wandering off and each time it does just follow it and bring it back to focusing on 'rising ... falling ... rising ...'

Don't give up. Even if you can only manage this meditation for a few minutes at a time, keep trying every day. It gets easier and easier and the reward of a calm mind is surely a priceless one!

Send your inner critic on holiday

56 Send Your Inner Critic on Holiday

Deep down we are all excessively self-critical, even the seemingly most confident people have a well-developed 'Inner Critic'. The inner critic is that part of each of us which nags away and is *never* satisfied with our performance. You can easily recognize its voice, it is the one which tells you off all the time; the one that keeps saying that you are never good enough/clever enough/thin enough/educated enough to do or be anything of note in this world.

It is important for us to understand that the inner critic will never be content because its work is never over: its job is to keep on criticizing and so it keeps us on the hook.

WAYS TO DEAL WITH THE INNER CRITIC

1 Accept that the inner critic will go on nagging at you.
2 Learn to recognize the voice of your inner critic. As soon as you start to feel low, listen to what you are saying to yourself. Are these negative things really true or is this the voice of your inner critic?
3 Visualize your inner critic resting in a deckchair, drink in hand, feet up in some exotic location. In other words, send your inner critic on holiday, keep him/her happy and he/she will stop telling you off.

Work on your inner critic in these three ways and soon you won't be continually bringing yourself down. You are an incredible and multi-talented person. Love and value yourself, be your own best friend, this amazing relationship will last for ever.

Create your own health farm

57 Create Your Own Health Farm

Allow yourself a whole day in which to enjoy a health-farm extravaganza in the privacy of your own home. Planning is important so decide beforehand exactly how you will spend your day.

Planning your day

- Buy any beauty items or toiletries that you might need. Choose your favourite treatments: mud masks; aroma-therapy oils for your bath; deep hair treatments; and anything else you would like to try but usually never have the time to.
- Choose some beautiful relaxing music and some aromatherapy oils to burn so that you can create an atmosphere of peace and tranquillity. Candlelight encourages relaxation so buy some candles if you haven't any.
- Choose a book or magazine to read. Get something that you really enjoy rather than something which you think would be 'good' for you to read. Remember this is *your* day to spend as *you* wish.
- Shop for some delicious nutritious food. Prepare it beforehand if you need to. Buy some pure fruit juice and bottled water to drink throughout the day (this helps to clear the mind and body of toxins).
- Get together anything else that you think you will need to complete your day of pampering.

Start your day by unplugging the phone and switching off TVs and computers.

When you spend a day just pampering yourself you will feel refreshed and invigorated. *When we learn to appreciate ourselves we are learning to appreciate our lives.*

Carpe Diem – seize the day

58 *Carpe Diem* – Seize the Day

This is it! This is another valuable moment of your precious life. This is not a dress rehearsal for the real thing, this *is* the performance of your life! Are you enjoying it?

We are not always able to appreciate the amazingness of life, our difficulties and defeats cloud our vision and so we often lose sight of the glory of it all. Look at a newborn baby, see the wonder in its eyes. You can still see the world in this way – the baby hasn't gone anywhere, she just grew up.

EXERCISE – THINGS I WOULD HAVE TO DO

If you were told that you had four weeks to live, what would you do immediately? What would you want to say to whom? What unfinished business would you be taking care of? Make a list of all the important things that you would feel you had to do.

* . . . .
* . . . .
* . . . .

We are not immortal, although we often live our lives as if we were. Take a look at the world as if you only had four weeks left – it looks different, doesn't it? *Seize the day*, today. Do what you know really needs doing. Live it dynamically, give it all you've got and just see what it gives back to you.

Be happy to do it

59 Be Happy to do it

We all know that the words we use affect the way that we feel. If we speak negatively we attract negativity and feel negative and the opposite is also true. Sometimes we use very small, seemingly innocuous words which can dramatically affect the quality of our lives.

I rang the information desk of a large company and the lady on the telephone was really helpful. Each time I asked her a question she said that she would find out but that she had 'got to' look on the computer screen/ask a colleague/ look up further details. This lady used the term 'got to' 5 times in 5 minutes. Now imagine that she is answering that busy helpline for 8 hours a day and every minute she says, 'I've got to …' – that's 480 'got tos' in one working day. I wonder how that lady feels at the end of her working day.

When we think we have 'got to' do something we put ourselves under pressure – just notice how you are feeling when you use that phrase. Well, after listening to this lady I became alerted to the potential power of 'got to' to ruin my day and I began to notice every time I said it. I felt rushed and resentful even as I said the words. So I started to use the words 'happy to do it' instead. I was running training courses with a friend at the time and we kept each other at it. One of us would say, 'I've got to move the chair/fill the kettle/complete this form … etc and the other one would change it to 'I'll be happy to …' (It's easier to recognize negative talk in others than to see it in ourselves.) We had such an hysterical time saying things like, 'I'll be happy to go to the toilet/go to the shop/move the flipchart/buy some paper/stick a stamp on the letter.' Why shouldn't we be happy doing even the simplest of things?

Watch your words, replace 'I've got to' with 'I'll be happy to' and you might even stop having headaches. I can guarantee that it will make you laugh and laugh and that in itself will make you feel great.

Never ever *give up*

60 Never *Ever* Give Up

When your life is hard and difficulties seem to appear whichever way you turn it is natural to feel dejected. When we are within the midst of a trauma we will not feel inclined to take helpful advice on how to 'feel better'. At this stage we really need to experience the power of our feelings of sadness, grief, anger, rage, hurt, shame or whatever other strong emotions we are feeling. However, the good news is that this immediate painful stage will pass. Everything changes, including our emotions. Remember that this is true and wait for that moment when your deep negativity begins to change. This change may begin in a very small way, in fact sometimes it is hardly recognizable. You may have been feeling very miserable and low for some time and then one day you sense a seed of hope. A client whose husband had died was very depressed for a couple of years. She said that she just felt that her life was meaningless and although she tried to pick up the pieces of her life she could never feel enthusiastic about anything. She dragged herself through her days and then one day in October she went to her grandson's Harvest Festival celebration at school. A very small girl with flowers in her hair sang the first verse of 'All Things Bright and Beautiful' and this lady said that it felt as though her heart moved. A spark of joy and hope was rekindled by this little girl and a healing process began.

The darkest light is truly just before the dawn. Never *ever* give up on the miraculous process of life. Believe in yourself, believe in the benevolence of the universe and know that you can and will feel hopeful and joyous again.